SPECIAL EFFECTS

Frances Ridley

 Crabtree Publishing Company

www.crabtreebooks.com

Crabtree Publishing Company

www.crabtreebooks.com   1-800-387-7650
Copyright © **2009 CRABTREE PUBLISHING COMPANY**.

**Published
in Canada
Crabtree Publishing**
616 Welland Ave.
St. Catharines, ON
L2M 5V6

**Published in the
United States
Crabtree Publishing**
PMB16A
350 Fifth Ave., Suite 3308
New York, NY 10118

Content development by Shakespeare Squared
www.ShakespeareSquared.com

With thanks to Ben Smith of Red Star Studio (3D Animation
and CGI Effects) and Mark Turner of MTFX Special Effects

Author: Frances Ridley
Project editor: Ruth Owen
Project designer: Simon Fenn
Photo research: Ruth Owen
Project coordinator: Robert Walker
Production coordinator: Katherine Berti
Prepress technicians: Samara Parent
    Katherine Berti, Ken Wright

Thank you to
Lorraine Petersen
and the members
of nasen

Picture credits:
Alamy: Photos 12: front cover
Corbis: Neal Preston: p. 14; Touchstone Pictures/ZUMA: p. 7
Corbis Sygma: Fox Anne Marie: p. 15; Pennington Donald: p. 24
Getty Images: p. 1, 18–19
MTFX Special Effects: p. 16, 17 (top right), 17 (top left), 20–21
Red Star Studio: p. 8–9
Rex Features: ©20th Century Fox/Everett: p. 4–5, 17 (bottom),
    22–23; ©BuenaVista/Everett: p. 11; Everett Collection: p. 28,
    29 (top); Jonathan Hordle: p. 6; SNAP: p. 29 (bottom);
    ©Universal/Everett: p. 13, 25, 31
Ronald Grant Archive: p. 10, 26, 27
Shutterstock: p. 2–3, 6 (background), 12, 26–27 (background)
www.jimusnr.com: p. 22 (top) (inset), 22 (bottom) (inset)

Every effort has been made to trace copyright holders, and we apologize in
advance for any omissions. We would be pleased to insert the appropriate
acknowledgments in any subsequent edition of this publication.

Library and Archives Canada Cataloguing in Publication

Ridley, Frances
    Special effects / Frances J. Ridley.

(Crabtree contact)
Includes index.
ISBN 978-0-7787-3824-4 (bound).--ISBN 978-0-7787-3845-9 (pbk.)

    1. Cinematography--Special effects--Juvenile literature.
I. Title. II. Series: Crabtree contact

TR858.R53 2009   j778.5'345   C2008-907894-2

Library of Congress Cataloging-in-Publication Data

Ridley, Frances.
    Special effects / Frances J. Ridley.
        p. cm. -- (Crabtree contact)
    Includes index.
    ISBN 978-0-7787-3845-9 (pbk. : alk. paper) -- ISBN
978-0-7787-3824-4 (reinforced library binding : alk. paper)
    1. Cinematography--Special effects--Juvenile literature. I. Title.

TR858.R54 2009
778.5'345--dc22

2008052418

CONTENTS

CHAPTER 1 MAKING IT REAL

What we see at the movies seems real.

We see fantastic creatures and terrible disasters.

We visit other times and other planets.

*Tornadoes rip through
Los Angeles, California, in the movie
The Day After Tomorrow*

We watch as people grow older
or change into horrible monsters.

But these **scenes** are not real.

They are made using special effects.

CHAPTER 2 CRAZY CREATURES

Many movie creatures are puppets.

Yoda was a tiny alien creature in the *Star Wars* movies.

In the *Star Wars* movie, *A New Hope*, the Yoda **character** was a hand puppet.

Yoda

How can you tell that Yoda is a puppet?

Yoda's eyes blink very slowly.
Yoda's lips do not move in time with the words.

The Vogons are huge aliens in the movie *The Hitchhiker's Guide to the Galaxy.*

Each Vogon is half puppet, half body suit.

The Vogon's head is **animatronic**. This means it has electronic machinery inside. A **puppeteer** makes the face move by remote control.

Animatronic Vogon head

The Vogon's body is hollow. The actor inside makes the Vogon walk.

Many modern films have **computer-generated** (CG) characters. Artists use computers to create them.

The artists collect information about the character. They decide what the character should look like. They find out how it should move and behave.

First, an artist draws a sketch of the character.

A wire frame model is created on a computer.

The artists draw the character on paper. Then the artists create the character on a computer screen.

The artists build the character up stage by stage.

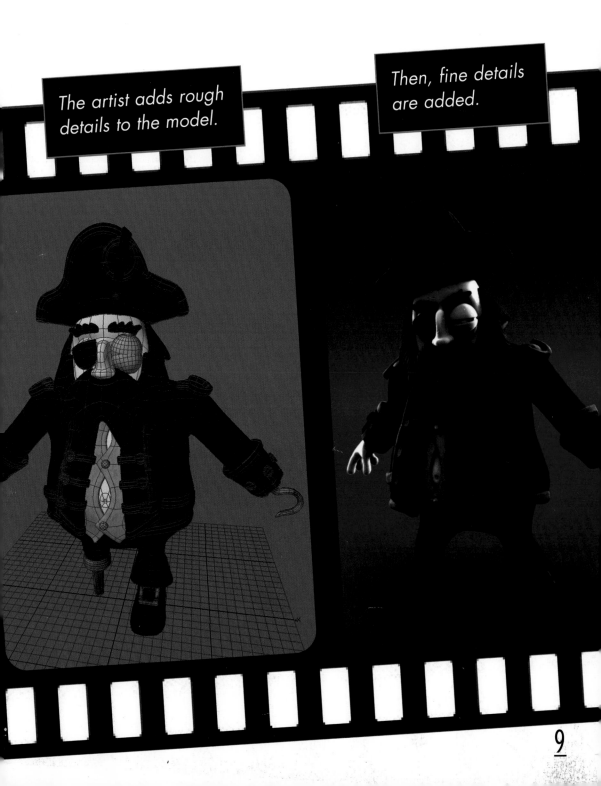

The artist adds rough details to the model.

Then, fine details are added.

Computer-generated characters are added to scenes after they have been filmed. The actors have to act with a character that isn't there.

This is a scene from *Harry Potter and the Prisoner of Azkaban*.

Buckbeak and Harry Potter

During filming, the actor, Daniel Radcliffe, had to pat a beak on a stick! The character Buckbeak was then added to the shot by computer.

In the movie, Harry Potter looks as if he is patting

Pip is a chipmunk in the movie *Enchanted*.
Pip is a CG character. Unlike a real chipmunk,
Pip can pull different faces.

During filming, a stuffed chipmunk was used to
show where the CG character would be.

Pip and Giselle in Enchanted

Trained animals and CG animals were used
in the *Harry Potter* movies and in *Enchanted*.

CHAPTER 3 | STRANGE CHANGES

Make-up artists change the way actors look.
They use effects such as fake blood and wigs.

Colored **contact lenses**

Make-up

False teeth

In the movie *Evan Almighty*, the main character starts out with short hair and no beard.

He changes to a man with flowing white hair and a beard!

The actor had to wear 19 different wigs and 17 beards.

The make-up artist carefully planned each stage of the change.

The make-up artist used a **technique** called "flocking." He stuck beard hairs on one at a time. This made it look as if the beard was growing out of the actor's face.

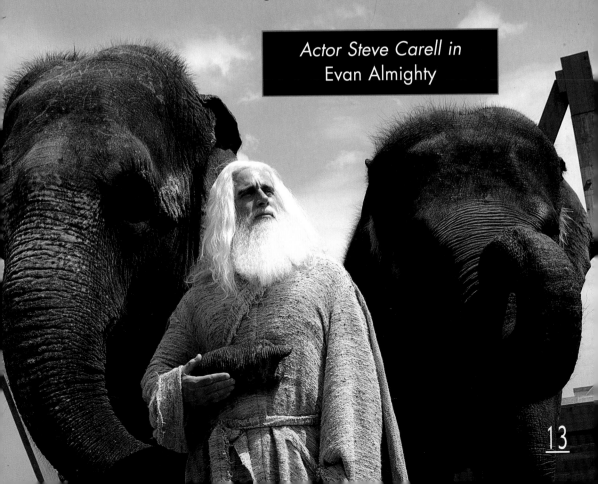

Actor Steve Carell in
Evan Almighty

Make-up artists use **prosthetic make-up** to create some effects. Masks and fake noses are both types of prosthetic make-up.

To make a prosthetic mask, the make-up artist first makes a plaster mold of the actor's face.

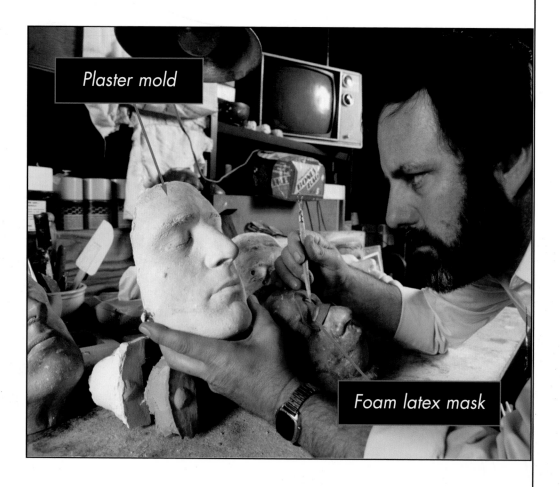

Plaster mold

Foam latex mask

The mold is used as a base to make a rubbery mask from **foam latex**. Effects such as scars, lumps, and warts can be added to the mask!

Then the mask is glued to the actor's face.

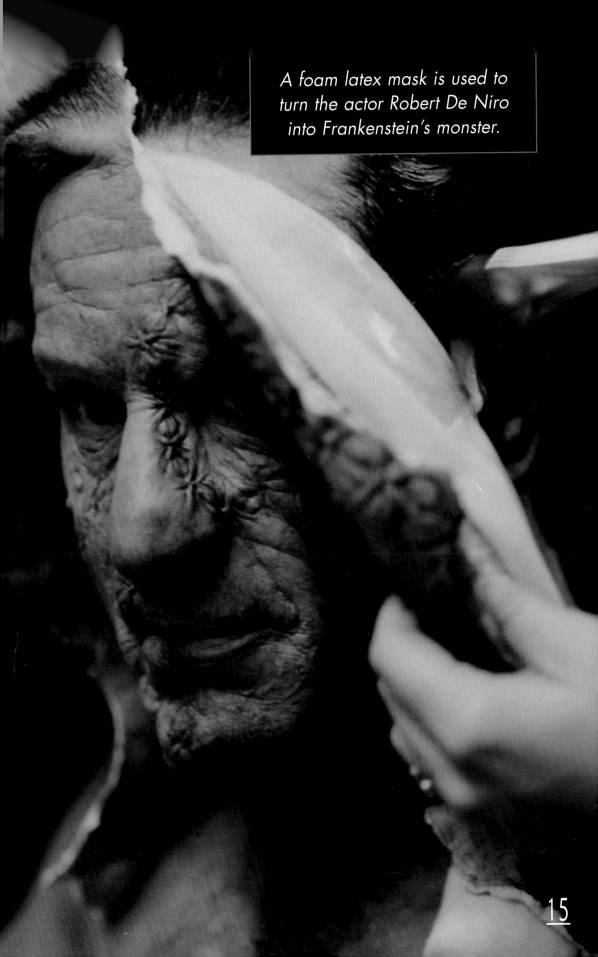

A foam latex mask is used to turn the actor Robert De Niro into Frankenstein's monster.

CHAPTER 4: BURNING BUILDINGS

There are fires and explosions in many action movies. It's dangerous to start a real fire on a film **set**. So, special effects are used instead.

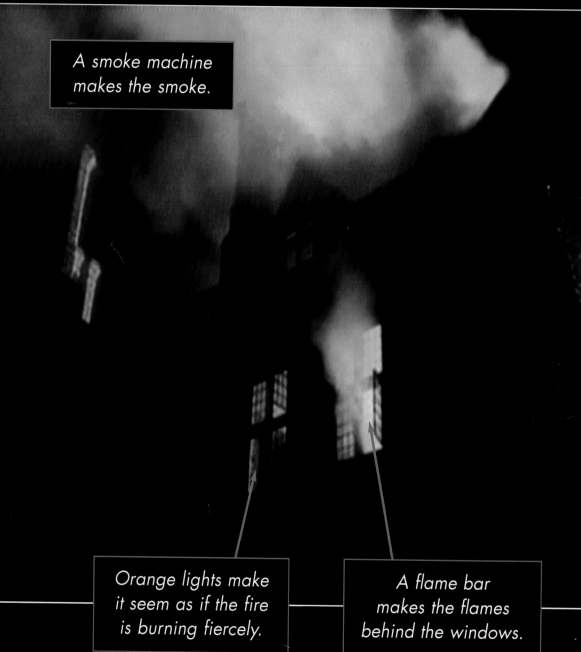

A smoke machine makes the smoke.

Orange lights make it seem as if the fire is burning fiercely.

A flame bar makes the flames behind the windows.

Flame bar

Smoke machine

A flame bar is a tube with holes in it. Gas bottles pump gas into the flame bar. Then the gas is set on fire to make a flame effect.

The Towering Inferno

Many scenes are filmed using models instead of real buildings or cars.

The burning skyscraper in the movie *The Towering Inferno* was a large model.

Special effects fires and explosions can be dangerous. They can also be very expensive.

Many modern movies now create these effects on computers.

The movie *Pearl Harbor* has scenes with fighter planes and explosions.

Some of the planes and explosions were real and some were computer generated.

Most movie-goers can't tell the difference!

Pearl Harbor

CHAPTER 5 STORMY WEATHER

Special effects teams often have to make the right weather for a movie.

Wind machine

A giant fan called a "wind machine" is used to make a gale.

A "rain stand" makes a rain effect.

Rain stands

A rain stand is like a big garden sprinkler. It's connected to a pump which is attached to a large container of water.

The pump pushes water through the rain stand at high pressure.

Some movie weather is really extreme!

In the movie *The Deluge*, New York is hit by
a tidal wave. The movie was made in 1933.

The special effects team built a huge model of New York.
Then they tipped tanks of water onto the model.

There is a tidal wave scene in *The Day After Tomorrow*.

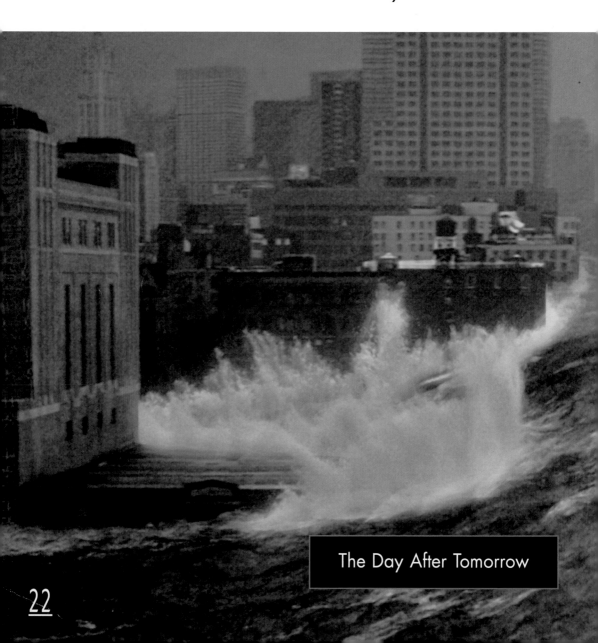

The Day After Tomorrow

The Day After Tomorrow was made in 2004.

The special effects team scanned 50,000 photos of New York into a computer. The photos were used to make a **digital model** of the city.

Then the city was destroyed by a digital wave!

A model of New York is covered in water in the movie The Deluge.

CHAPTER 6

SETTING THE SCENE

Movies can be set in castles, spaceships, or on boats. The 1997 movie *Titanic* was set onboard a giant ocean liner.

The special effects team built a **scale model** of the Titanic. The model is one twentieth of the size of the real ship. It is almost 46 feet (14 m) long.

The model took 65 model-makers almost five months to create.

The *Titanic model*

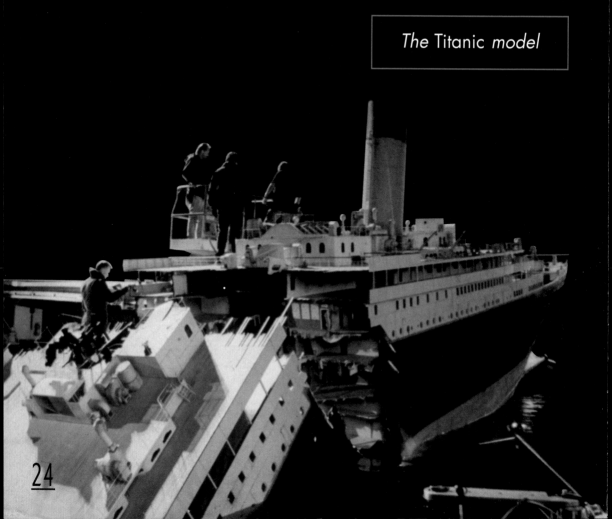

In the movie *Evan Almighty*, God tells the main character to build an ark, or giant boat, just like Noah does in the Bible.

The movie-makers built an ark that was over 450 feet (137 m) long!

The ark from Evan Almighty

The background scenery in movies is often not real. It can be a painted scene or a scene created on a computer. This is called matte painting.

In the past, backgrounds were painted on glass. Then the painting was filmed.

The actors were filmed against a blue background.

Then the two films were put together to make one piece of film.

Blue screen background

In modern films, the backgrounds are created on computers.

The actors are filmed against a blue or green screen.

Then the two images are put together using computers.

Computer generated background

CHAPTER 7

TIMELINE

1895 - The Execution of Mary, Queen of Scots

This movie featured the first ever special effect. In the movie, a character was **executed**. A dummy was used for the scene.

1933 - King Kong

This was the first *King Kong* movie. The special effects team used a model gorilla, model sets, and a doll.

1963 - Jason and the Argonauts

Fighting skeletons were brought to life using stop-motion in this movie. Many photographs were taken of the models at different stages of movement. Then, the pictures were run together very fast.

In this movie, a giant alien spaceship lands on Earth. The spaceship was a six-and-a-half-foot (2 m) wide model.

1995 - Toy Story

Toy Story was the first completely computer generated movie.

NEED-TO-KNOW WORDS

animatronic Puppets that have electronic machinery inside them. A puppeteer makes the puppet move by remote control

character A person, animal, or creature in the story of a film, book, or TV show

computer generated (CG) Something that is created on a computer. A computer artist puts information about a character or background into a computer. The artist then creates a picture of the character or background on screen

contact lens A small piece of plastic that is put on the surface of the eye. Contact lenses help people to see clearly. Some contact lenses are in different colors. They can change the color of the eyes

digital model A picture on a computer screen that looks 3D

executed When a person is put to death

foam latex A man-made material that can be molded easily when it is wet. Special effects make-up artists use it to make masks and to create 3D make-up effects

prosthetic make-up 3D make-up that changes the shape of an actor's face or body

puppeteer A person who makes a puppet move

scale model A copy of an object that is smaller than the real object

scene A small part of a film that is set in one time and place. When the time and place changes, another scene begins

set The background in a movie or TV scene. For example, it might look as if the actors in a movie are in their kitchen at home. In fact, the kitchen is a set that has been built in a movie studio

technique A way of doing something

SPECIAL EFFECTS FIRSTS

- The first ever Academy Award, or Oscar, for make-up was given in 1981. It went to special effects make-up artist Rick Baker. He won it for his work on the movie *An American Werewolf in London.*

- The first movie to include a fully CG character was *Young Sherlock Holmes.* The movie was made in 1985. The CG character is a knight who is part of a stained glass window. The knight comes to life and jumps out of the window.

- The first movie to use live actors and all CG sets was *Sky Captain and the World of Tomorrow.* It was made in 2004.

An American Werewolf in London

SPECIAL EFFECTS ONLINE

www.pbs.org/wgbh/nova/specialfx2/
Includes a special effects timeline and glossary

videos.howstuffworks.com/reuters/3358-beowulf-3-d-technology-video.htm
Videos showing how special effects are created

INDEX

Printed in the U.S.A. - BG